Samuel French Acting Edition

The Revenge of the Red Feather Ladies

by Maxine Holmgren

SAMUELFRENCH.COM   SAMUELFRENCH.CO.UK

Copyright © 2006, 2007 by Maxine Holmgren
All Rights Reserved

THE REVENGE OF THE RED FEATHER LADIES is fully protected under the copyright laws of the United States of America, the British Commonwealth, including Canada, and all other countries of the Copyright Union. All rights, including professional and amateur stage productions, recitation, lecturing, public reading, motion picture, radio broadcasting, television and the rights of translation into foreign languages are strictly reserved.

ISBN 978-0-874-40010-6

www.SamuelFrench.com
www.SamuelFrench.co.uk

FOR PRODUCTION ENQUIRIES
UNITED STATES AND CANADA
Info@SamuelFrench.com
1-866-598-8449
UNITED KINGDOM AND EUROPE
Plays@SamuelFrench.co.uk
020-7255-4302

Each title is subject to availability from Samuel French, depending upon country of performance. Please be aware that *THE REVENGE OF THE RED FEATHER LADIES* may not be licensed by Samuel French in your territory. Professional and amateur producers should contact the nearest Samuel French office or licensing partner to verify availability.

CAUTION: Professional and amateur producers are hereby warned that *THE REVENGE OF THE RED FEATHER LADIES* is subject to a licensing fee. Publication of this play(s) does not imply availability for performance. Both amateurs and professionals considering a production are strongly advised to apply to Samuel French before starting rehearsals, advertising, or booking a theatre. A licensing fee must be paid whether the title(s) is presented for charity or gain and whether or not admission is charged. Professional/Stock licensing fees are quoted upon application to Samuel French.

No one shall make any changes in this title(s) for the purpose of production. No part of this book may be reproduced, stored in a retrieval system, or transmitted in any form, by any means, now known or yet to be invented, including mechanical, electronic, photocopying, recording, videotaping, or otherwise, without the prior written permission of the publisher. No one shall upload this title(s), or part of this title(s), to any social media websites.

For all enquiries regarding motion picture, television, and other media rights, please contact Samuel French.

Please refer to page 27 for further copyright information.

The Revenge of the Red Feather Ladies was originally produced by the Sun City Players, Gene Dudek, President, on June 10-11, 2006. The production was under the direction of Maxine Holmgren with the following cast:

BETTY	Betty Jo Adney
ALICE	Jo Bushnell
LOUISE	Pat Mogge
JANE	Donna Ogier
BARBARA	Diane Coombs
ROSEANN	Marcia Stroope
CHARLENE	Susan Carreiro

CHARACTERS

BETTY - The Prime Plume of the Red Feather Ladies Investment Club. She is a retired attorney. She is suspicious of everything and everyone.

LOUISE - A fun loving, adventurous member of the Red Feather group. A former cheer leader, she is always cheerful. Tends to be loud and brash.

CHARLENE - A shy, quiet, studious member of the group. She is not very well coordinated and is prone to dropping things, knocking things over and bumping into things.

BARBARA - A pill popping hypochondriac. She always has health problems but looks the picture of health and never misses a meeting.

JANE - A sophisticated socialite member. Her position in society is very important to her. She is very dramatic and demonstrative in her manner of speech.

ROSEANN - Is from the South, and speaks with a Southern drawl. She is a sweet, naïve member of the Red Feather Investment Club.

(All of these characters wear something with a large red feather. It could be on a hat, purse, boa, or any accessory.)

WAITRESS - Wears typical waitress outfit. She is not too bright. She reads her greeting each time she says it.

SETTING

The play takes place in a tea room. There is a door to the outside on stage right, a door to the kitchen on stage left. A long table and chairs are center stage, smaller tables set for tea guests are also on stage. The room should be decorated as a typical tea room, very feminine. There are pretty floral pictures and arrangements on the walls. A large easel is on one side of the stage or on the apron of the stage. A poster with the tea room name sits on it. This should also be decorated with flowers. A clock is on the wall.

(AT RISE: We see BETTY seated at the middle of the table, studying a menu. She is waiting impatiently for the others. She taps her fingers, looks at her watch, rolls her eyes, etc.)

WAITRESS. *(ENTERS from kitchen. Has order pad in hand, approaches BETTY. Does not look at BETTY. Reads from order pad.)* Hello. My name is Alice. I'll be your server today. Are you ready to order?

BETTY. Do I look like I'm ready to order? I'm all alone at a table for six. Of course I'm not ready to order. I'm waiting for five other people. Is that clock right?

WAITRESS. *(Looking puzzled.)* I don't know. No one's ever asked me that before. Should I go ask the manager?

BETTY. Never mind. Just bring me some water.

WAITRESS. With ice or without?

BETTY. I don't care, just bring it!

WAITRESS. I think there's more room for water without the ice in the glass.

BETTY. Fine. Without ice. *(Looks at watch again.)*

WAITRESS. But it stays colder with ice.

BETTY. *(Glares at WAITRESS.)* Just bring me a glass of water — without ice.

(WAITRESS EXITS. BETTY takes out large framed photo from her brief case, looks at it, smiles, plants a kiss on it, returns to brief case.)

LOUISE. *(LOUISE ENTERS. Smiling, happy, loud. Waves boa in greeting.)* Hi ya, Betty! Oh, good. I thought I was late but I'm the first one! I love being first.

(Hugs BETTY then sits, leaving empty chair between her and BETTY.)

BETTY. You're not the first, I am. And everyone, including you, is late — as usual.
LOUISE. Well, it was kind of short notice. You calling this meeting, I mean. You said it was a special meeting, 'cause you had something important to share with us. I hope it's some good news. 'Cause I have some good news too. I can't wait to tell everyone. Oh, look here's Jane.
JANE. *(JANE ENTERS. JANE makes a dramatic entrance. Pauses at door, looks around room. Walks slowly, as if on parade, to table and sits between BETTY and LOUISE. Very snobbish.)* Hello, darlings. Sorry to be late, Madam Prime Plume, but I just came from another social engagement. It was very difficult, you know, for me to clear my calendar for this unscheduled meeting. In fact, the only reason I accommodated your impromptu event, was because I have news to share of the utmost importance.
LOUISE. What fun! I do, too!
WAITRESS. *(WAITRESS ENTERS. Keeps her eyes on order pad.)* Hello, my name is Alice. I'll be your server today. Are you ready to order?

THE REVENGE OF THE RED FEATHER LADIES

BETTY. No, we are not ready to order! There are only three of us, at a table for six.

LOUISE. I could use some water, please.

WAITRESS. With or without ice?

BETTY. Oh no, not again! Bring all of us some water — without ice.

WAITRESS. *(Counts ladies at table.)* That would be three glasses of water without ice. I better write that down.

(EXITS as she is writing.)

BETTY. Maybe this time she'll actually bring it.

BARBARA. *(BARBARA ENTERS, walks stooped over.)* Hello everyone. I'd have been here sooner, but my arthritis is acting up so bad, I could hardly get dressed. *(She plops down, next to JANE.)* I'll just sit here. I can't go any farther.

(Takes out pill bottles and lines them up.)

WAITRESS. *(WAITRESS ENTERS. Carries tray with 3 glasses of water — with ice. Serves BETTY, LOUISE and JANE. Then notices BARBARA. Reads:)* Oh, hello. My name is Alice. I'll be your server today. Are you ready to order?

BARBARA. I just barely sat down. I haven't even seen the menu. But I'd like some water, I have to take my medication.

WAITRESS. With or without ice?

BETTY. Here we go again. *(Raises glass and tinkles ice.)* Maybe if you order it with ice, you'll get it without.

BARBARA. No ice. It will give me a headache. In fact, I feel one coming on now. I need water right away.

(WAITRESS EXITS, writing on her pad.)

JANE. Here, dear, Have my water. I only drink fresh bottled spring water. You can take the ice out. *(Takes fancy bottled water from her purse. ROSEANN and CHARLENE ENTER together. ROSEANN has to pull CHARLENE along.)*

ROSEANN. H'lo, ya all. I saw Charlene standing outside; I think she was afraid to enter by herself, so I brought her right in.

(Sits next to LOUISE.)

CHARLENE. *(CHARLENE ENTERS shyly, adjusting her glasses, clutching her purse and some books.)* "I just wasn't sure if this was the right place. I didn't want to make a mistake."

ROSEANN. You're such a silly. Betty told us to meet at the Fancy Frills Tea Room on the corner of Bradley and Cherry Hills Blvd. Do you see any other Tea Room on the corner?

CHARLENE. *(Drops book as she speaks.)* I'm glad you came along and knew just where to go.

WAITRESS. *(Hurries in with water for BARBARA.)* Here's your water, Ma'm. For your medication-*(Stops as she sees BARBARA already has water.)* Oh, you have water. Did I already bring you water? *(Confused)* I guess I forgot.

JANE. *(Condescending)* No, my dear. I gave her mine. I don't drink plain water.

WAITRESS. What should I do with this? *(Holds up glass of water with ice.)*

JANE. Why don't you drink it, dear.

WAITRESS. Yes, Ma'm. *(Drinks water then notices ROSEANN and CHARLENE. Puts glass down and counts guests. Gets out her order pad and reads:)* Hello, My name is Alice. I'll be your server for the day. Are you ready to order?

BETTY. Yes, Alice. We are ready to order. *(Stands)* As the Prime Plume of the Red Feather Ladies Investment Club, I have made an executive decision. I propose that we all order the same thing, the Queen's Royal Tea. It includes scones, tea sandwiches and desert for $17.50. All in favor – say Aye.

(All say aye except for BARBARA.)

BARBARA. Well, I don't know. Do the tea sandwiches have shellfish in them? I'm allergic to shellfish.

BETTY. *(Reading from the menu.)* Chicken salad, egg salad and cucumber tea sandwiches.

BARBARA. Ooooh, that's a lot of mayonnaise. I have to watch my cholesterol, you know. And the desert? Any peanuts? When I eat peanuts I break out into a terrible rash...

BETTY. No, I'm sure crème puffs don't have peanuts in them.

BARBARA. Well, alright. I don't want to be difficult. I should have just brought my health food bars to eat. They're full of protein, you know.

BETTY. *(To WAITRESS as she sits down.)* We'll all have the Queen's Royal Tea, please.

WAITRESS. Is that for here or to go?

BETTY. *(Exasperated)* It's for here! Do you think we're in a drive through? Just go get our food! And put it all on one ticket and give the bill to me. *(Turning to girls.)* This one's on the Investment Club, girls. It comes under the category of a Special Business Meeting. I know you're all wondering why I called you all together like this. Well, I have such good news, of a personal nature, I just couldn't wait till our next meeting to tell you.

LOUISE. *(Excited, she stands.)* That's great, Betty, but I have news too. As President, I mean Prime Plume, you always get to go first. I just have to tell you my news first. Look, everyone, I'm engaged.

(Stands and holds out her hand, so everyone can see her engagement ring.)

JANE. *(All together.)* How marvelous for you, darling.
BARBARA. Well, What do you know! Good for you. I hope he's in good health.
CHARLENE. Congratulations. How nice for you.

(Knocks over empty cup as she extends hand to shake LOUISE'S hand.)

ROSEANN. Congratulations. Who's the lucky fella? Tell us everything. Then I have something to tell you too.
LOUISE. His name is Willy Waterman, and what a hunk! He's tall, dark and handsome — and oozing charm from every pore of his beautiful body.
CHARLENE. *(Blushing)* Oh, my! Please, Louise, must you be so descriptive?
LOUISE. I met him one evening when I was coming home from the Red Feather Investment Club meeting down at the big hotel on the corner. I heard music coming from the

hotel lounge, and well, you know me, I couldn't resist! I just had to stop in and see what band was playing. So, I found a table and ordered a drink.

JANE. *(With disdain.)* Don't tell me you let a strange man pick you up! How common! Really, Louise, I'm surprised at your behavior.

LOUISE. *(Ignoring her.)* Next thing I know, this gorgeous hunk of a man comes up to me and asks me to dance. *(Bounce up and down, wave boa in excitement.)* He used that old line "What's a pretty girl like you, in such a pretty red hat, doing in a place like this, all alone?" *(Giggles)* Just then I had a hot flash, and I thought I was gonna molt red feathers all over the place. I told him I was on my way home from my Investment Club, and he tells me he's a big investment consultant and he'd be happy to give me some advice.

BETTY. Sounds like a fast talker to me. You better be careful. Anyway, as I was about to tell you my good news-

JANE. *(Interrupts)* But I have something really important to tell my fine red feathered friends. I want to tell you before you read it in the society column. *(She holds forth her hand to show ring.)* I, too, am engaged!

BETTY. *(All together.)* Oh, my goodness. Congratulations.

CHARLENE. *(All together.)* Congratulations.

BARBARA. *(All together.)* How nice.

LOUISE. *(All together.)* You, too? Congratulations, honey.

ROSEANN. And how did you meet your fiancé?

JANE. I met Willard at the Fund Raising Ball for the Socially Challenged. Tickets were $200 each, you know. I had just been seated and was arranging my cape on the back of my chair. I was wearing the black velvet one with the red feather trim. Well, to make a long story short, my diamond bracelet became entangled in the feathers, and dear Willard came to my assistance. Most gallant of him, I thought. Well, he sat next to me, and we talked and talked all evening. *(Smugly)* He said it was so nice to talk to a woman who actually understood stocks and bonds and investments. Thanks to our Red Feather Investment Club, I even knew about the gold market...

LOUISE. Hmmm, sounds like a pick-up to me.

JANE. *(Stands, in anger.)* How dare you! Don't even begin to compare my Willard with your Willy Waterman! Willard is tall, dark and handsome, but believe me, he's a true gentleman, not a lounge lizard!.

LOUISE. *(Starts to rise.)* Now, listen here, you —

BETTY. Now, girls, behave yourselves. Let's just be happy for each other. And here come the scones!

WAITRESS. Hello, My name is Alice. I'm serving your scones today.

(Serves scones and tea and EXITS.)

BARBARA. *(Fanning herself.)* I can feel my blood pressure rising. If I don't tell you my news pretty soon, I may have a stroke. I don't care what the proper order of business is at this meeting, I have to tell you. I'm gonna get married! There, I said it!

(All together:)

    ROSEANN. You, too? How wonderful!
    CHARLENE. Congratulations.

(Struggle taking off jacket, boa or shawl.)

JANE. Really? How unusual. Oh — congratulations.

LOUISE. Good for you. Another pick up?

BETTY. I may as well give up trying to speak. Congratulations, Barbara. Tell us all about him. Is he a Doctor?

BARBARA. I met William at the pharmacy. I was getting several of my prescriptions refilled, and when he noticed how many I was taking and the exorbitant cost of them, he became very concerned. He was such a gentleman — he insisted on walking me to my car, and followed me home to make sure I didn't faint on the way there. Then, a few days later, he stopped by to see how I was doing. He took such an interest in my health.

BETTY. That's rather strange.

BARBARA. I told him all about my operations, and the pain I had in my chest. And when he heard I had no family, no one to look after me, he felt so sorry for me. *(Fanning)* My, it's hot in here. He sympathized with me that the only activity I could still enjoy was watching my investments grow in the Red Feather Investment Club.

BETTY. And I suppose he's old and fat and bald?

BARBARA. No, quite the contrary. I wish I had a picture of him. *(Mop forehead.)* He never wanted his picture taken. Says he's not very photogenic. Neither am I, really, and I wonder about those flash bulbs. Seems to me that they could damage your retinas.

JANE. I quite understand his position. My Willard does not like to have his photo taken either. We were at a fund raising dinner for the Rich and Feeble, and I wanted our picture taken for the society page, and Willard refused. Quite adamantly, I might add. Something about being humble. I didn't understand at all, but I thought oh well. Come ci, come ca.

ROSEANN. *(Jumps up.)* I can't keep still another minute! Look, y'all! I'm engaged too!

(All together.)

    BETTY. Oh, no, not another! What's going on?
    CHARLENE. Congratulations.
    LOUISE. Congrats, honey!
    JANE. Really? How nice. I mean, Congratulations.
    BARBARA. Where's my antacid? Oh, yes, congratulations, RoseAnn.

(WAITRESS ENTERS to clear scones and EXITS.)

    BETTY. Go on, tell us all about your Prince Charming. I know you're going to, so I won't try to stop you. Even though I'm the one who called this meeting.
    ROSEANN. I'm sorry, Betty. I just couldn't keep it to myself another minute. Well, I met Wilson a few months ago at the Kentucky Derby. It was a hot day and I was fanning myself with that fan we all got from the Red Feather Investment Club Summer Party. Y'all know the one I mean, the one with the red feathers on it. Well, Wilson noticed me, and offered to get me a cool drink. He's such a gentleman. He said he knew right away that I came from the finest breeding stock in Kentucky.

(CHARLENE gasps in shock. WAITRESS ENTERS to serve sandwiches. Almost drops tray in shock.)

ROSEANN. I mean, our horses come from the finest breeding stock, and since I own half the stables with Daddy, oh — ya'all know what I mean. Well, Wilson and I just hit it off right away. He started courting me, and next thing I knew, we were engaged! *(Shows off flashy diamond ring.)* We went dancin' and dinin' — I just live for Friday nights. He's out of town on business the rest of the week, you see.

LOUISE. Ain't that a drag though! I know just how you feel, dearie. My Willy's gone a lot on business too. We only get together on Mondays. What a bummer. But he's worth waitin' for.

BETTY. Alright! If you're all done talking about your love life, may I share my important news now? Or do you have a Romeo in your life too, Charlene?

(Everyone laughs.)

BARBARA. "That'll be the day!"
LOUISE. "Who, her?"
JANE. "That bookworm."
CHARLENE. *(Shyly)* Well, as a matter of fact, I do have something to tell you. I know that you all think that all I ever do is sit around and read books. Well, I'll have you know one day I got brave and I joined a club.

ROSEANN. We don't think that at all, sweetie. What kind of club did you join?

CHARLENE. I joined a chat club on the internet. *(Warming to her subject.)* It was really quite exciting. I met the most interesting people. One of them was a man who called himself "Billy, the Kid." I started chatting back and forth with him. Of course, he wasn't really a kid. You've probably heard of internet romance? Well, we fell in love on the internet.

ROSEANN. Did you ever meet him?

CHARLENE. Yes! Oh, I know it was fate. I just happened to mention in the chat room that the apartments I owned had a vacancy. I told them how I had bought them at a great price through the Red Feather Investment Club. Billy inquired about them, and when I told him they were the upscale apartments on Snooty Ave., he was thrilled. It seems he had been looking for a new apartment. He asked if we could meet so he could see the apartment.

ROSEANN. And when you met, was it love at first sight?

CHARLENE. Yes, he loved the apartment.

LOUISE. Forget the apartment! What about you two?

CHARLENE. My goodness, what a meeting that was! I told him I'd be wearing a red feather so he'd recognize me. He was so charming, everything I've always looked for in a man. Well, one thing led to another, and before I knew it we were seeing each other every Tuesday night. He travels a lot the rest of the time, you see, doing humanitarian work. But he emails me every day.

BETTY. Do you have a picture of him?

CHARLENE. He gave me one of himself when he came back from his last mission trip to Africa. He had a full beard and long hair. It didn't even look like him. He's really very good looking. Tall, dark hair — and so polite and considerate. He's so worried about the money he owes me for back rent.

THE REVENGE OF THE RED FEATHER LADIES

But I keep telling him, not to worry. I know he'll pay me as soon as his money gets transferred from that bank in Africa. They're so backward down there, you know. It takes a long, long time.

ROSEANN. Well, I think that's just wonderful, sugar!
LOUISE. I never thought you had it in you!

(CHARLENE drops fork or spoon.)

BETTY. *(Stands, clutching framed photo to her chest, hiding picture.)* Well, if you're all finished congratulating yourselves on being engaged, I have some real news. I am happy to announce that the Prime Plume of the Red Feather Ladies Investment Club — that's me — has snagged the best deal of all. I have met the most amazing man. I met Bill at the courthouse. I was searching some court records, as I like to do in my spare time. Bill was there looking up some real estate records. We started talking, and when it was lunch time, he invited me to go to the courthouse cafeteria with him. That was the beginning of our whirlwind romance. We saw each other every Saturday night. The rest of the week he was away on business. He's building a shopping mall in the Mojave Desert. There's no traffic congestion there, you know, so Bill is convinced it will make it easier for shoppers to get there. He's so smart — and handsome. Anyway — next week we're going to get married!

(All at once :)

BARBARA. Congratulations!
ROSEANN. I love it!

LOUISE. It must be contagious! Congrats!
CHARLENE. Congratulations.
JANE. How mahvelous!
BETTY. And I can do more than any of you could do! *(Triumphantly)* I have a picture of my fiancé!

(Walks slowly down the line, showing picture to each one. She stands in back and to the right of each one. As each one reacts, she then moves on to the next one.)

BARBARA. *(Reacting in horror.)* Oh! Oh! No, it can't be! That's a picture of my William! No!

(Clutches chest and faints back in chair. BETTY moves on, showing picture to JANE.)

JANE. *(Looking at BARBARA.)* What on earth is wrong? *(Looks at picture.)* That picture! Why — why — it's none other than my fiancé, Willard. How did you get his picture?
BETTY. This is MY fiancé, Bill. What do you mean, your fiancé?
JANE. That's Willard! Oh, dear, you mean — you mean he's engaged to the three of us? This is terrible! Oh, my, what will my friends at the Country Club say?

(BETTY moves on, showing the picture to LOUISE.)

LOUISE. Hey! That's a picture of Willy! I'd know that mug anywhere. I ain't never seen him dressed up in a business suit like that, but it's him alright. What's he trying to pull? What's going on here anyway?

(BETTY shows picture to ROSEANN.)

ROSEANN. Calm down, honey child. I'm sure there's an explanation. *(Looks at picture.)* Lands sake alive — it's my dahlin' Wilson! Wilson, how could you betray me like this? You said I was your only true love.

CHARLENE. That's exactly what Billy told me! Oh, I'm afraid to look at that picture. *(Hands over eyes.)*

BETTY. *(Moving on to CHARLENE.)* Open your eyes, Charlene. Maybe it's not your boyfriend after all.

CHARLENE. *(Opens eyes, looks at picture.)* It's him. *(Starts to cry.)* It's Billy. How can Billy be your fiancé? And hers, and hers, and hers? *(Pointing to others.)*

BARBARA. And mine too. I'm shocked. *(Start taking pills.)*

BETTY. You're shocked! How do you think I feel? I call this meeting to tell you that I am getting married next week, and moving to the desert and that you'll have to find a new President Plume and before I know it, you all tell me you're engaged. And it turns out you're all engaged to the same man! My fiancé! And I call myself a criminal lawyer? *(Sits down again.)* Retired, of course.

BARBARA. I should have known it was too good to be true!

LOUISE. I've read about those guys that lead double lives. He was just playin' all of us for our money!

WAITRESS. Hope you're finished.

(Removes plates while they are still eating & EXITS.)

JANE. Oh, this is just terrible. What will I tell my friends at the country club?

CHARLENE. Do you mean he never intended to pay me the money he owed me?

BETTY. Sorry, Charlene. It looks like he was up to no good all the time he was seeing you. Seeing all of us, I mean.

BARBARA. And I thought he was just being considerate when he took out insurance policies on both of us. But I wondered why he took out $500,000 on me and only $50,000 on him.

CHARLENE. *(Still tearful.)* We were going to go to Hawaii on our honeymoon. He was going to take me sailing. I told him I was afraid of getting sea-sick, but he said I wouldn't be on the boat that long and didn't have to worry about it. *(Suddenly seeing the light.)* Oh! Do you think he intended to throw me overboard? *(Starts wailing again.)*

JANE. How awful! You know, now that I think about it – I wondered why he only took me out on Thursday evenings. Such a dull evening, social wise, you know. But now I understand. He was with someone else every other night of the week.

LOUISE. Mondays.

CHARLENE. Tuesdays.

BARBARA. Wednesdays.

JANE. Thursdays.

ROSEANN. Fridays.

BETTY. Saturdays. He must have seen the movie, "Never on Sundays."

JANE. He was going to take me to a Swiss chalet on our honeymoon. I told him I wasn't much of an outdoor girl, but he said he couldn't wait to take me mountain climbing. Oh, my, do you think he intended-oh, dear!

(WAITRESS ENTERS to serve desert.)

WAITRESS. Crème puffs are our specialty, I think.

BARBARA. Oh, dear! Look at that desert. My cholesterol will rise 10 points, I'm sure. I better take another pill. *(Proceeds to do so.)*

BETTY. The plot thickens! He not only was engaged to all of us, it looks like he was planning on doing away with us.

ROSEANN. No wonder he never wanted his picture taken! He was afraid of being recognized. How did you manage to get that picture, Betty?

BETTY. It wasn't easy. He refused to have his photo taken at a courthouse picnic we attended and that upset me. He tried to pass it off as a joke — saying he was too sunburned from being out at the desert mall the day before. So I had one of my retired detective friends take his picture when he wasn't aware of it.

CHARLENE. You're a lawyer, Betty. What should we do? Should we call the police? Should we report him as a botamist?

LOUISE. You mean bigotrist.

BETTY. You both mean bigamist! But he hasn't actually married anyone yet.

JANE. The police! Oh, no! My name musn't be mentioned in the newspapers! The notoriety would kill me!

ROSEANN. Better the notoriety kill you than that mountain climbing murderer.

LOUISE. Well, I don't know what the rest of you are gonna do, but I know what I'm gonna do! I don't often talk about it, but I have a cousin who's got connections with the mafia. He said if I every needed anything, I should give him a call. 'Scuse me, girls *(Gets up from table.)* I've got a phone call to make. *(Leaves table. EXITS.)*

ROSEANN. Well, we Southerners have a way of taking care of our own. I'm gonna call my brother. When he finds out that dirty rat has deceived his little baby sister, he'll take care of him for me. *(Stands)* My brother is an I.R.S. agent, you see. He can fix it so Wilson won't be seeing anyone but prison guards for the next ten or fifteen years. Where's my cell phone? *(Leaves table, digging in purse for phone EXITS.)*

JANE. Well, I'm not going to leave it up to chance. I can't afford to take any chances that this is going to be exposed in the newspapers. I'm going to hire a — *(Searching for right word.)* a — a — security guard. Yes, that's it. A security guard to guard my social standing. To make sure it is secure. Someone to apply a little pressure to our collective fiancé, and make sure he leaves town. In fact, I'm going to do it right now! *(EXITS.)*

BETTY. Looks like Willy, Bill, Willard — whatever alias he goes by is in for trouble.

CHARLENE. I don't know how those girls can think of resorting to violence.

BARBARA. I agree! I have a much better plan. Over the years, I've become good friends with the pharmacist. I'm going to get him to give me some pills that induce violent vomiting and diarrhea. Then I'll visit William one more time, and slip them to him. He'll be too pooped to party with anyone for quite some time! *(Start putting pill bottles in purse, getting ready to leave.)*

CHARLENE. *(Making a face.)* Ooo, that's disgusting. I have a better idea. I've become pretty good on the computer you know. I've even learned some tricks. I think I'll just find his on-line banking account and transfer all his money into my account. After I max out his credit cards, of course. Come on, Barbara, this could be fun!

(BARBARA and CHARLENE EXIT. CHARLENE almost knocks over chair, drops book on way out. BETTY is alone at table. She takes out photo and gazes at it. Then plants another kiss on it.)

BETTY. Well, Bill, looks like it's just you and me now. You're going to need someone to comfort you. I'm afraid you may be in for a bit of a rough time in the future, but don't you worry. I'll defend you. Now that I've got you ALL TO MYSELF!

CURTAIN CLOSES

COSTUME PLOT

BETTY - A business suit such as a retired professional might wear. She should have a hat with a very large red feather(s) appropriate to her title of the Prime Plume of the Red Feather Ladies Investment Club. She wears a showy engagement ring. Carries a brief case with 8X10 picture of a man.

LOUISE - Loud, brightly colored mini dress or tight fitting capris and top. She wears red feathered boa, lots of jewelry and a flashy engagement ring.

CHARLENE - Plain, neutral colored outfit. She has a large red feather pinned to her lapel. She wears glasses, and carries a purse. Wears engagement ring. Carries too many books, note pads, etc.

BARBARA - Layers of sweaters, scarves, hat with red feather. Plain walking shoes. Carries a large purse full of pill bottles and fan. Uses a cane or walker. Wears engagement ring.

JANE - Attractive, expensive looking dress, suit or pant suit. Large pieces of jewelry to denote wealth, very large engagement ring. Wears a hat with red feathers, carries expensive looking purse that contains fancy water bottle.

ROSEANN - A summery, frilly dress, with lots of lace and ruffles, floppy sun hat with red feather attached. Wears engagement ring.

WAITRESS - Typical waitress outfit, with tea apron. Carries an order pad, pencil and card from which she reads her greeting.

SET PLOT

Interior scene of Fancy Frills Tea Room
Kitchen is stage left
Outside door is stage right
Set and walls are decorated with floral arrangements, vintage collectables, candles, teapots, etc.

PROPERTY PLOT
PRESET

(Center)
Long table with 6 chairs, four facing audience and one at each end. Tablecloth
Table settings for six (plates, silverware, cups, napkins)
Creamer and sugar Jam, lemon curd for scones

(Stage left)
Small ice cream table and chairs, set for tea
Door to kitchen

(Stage right)
Easel holding poster with name "Fancy Frills Tea Room".
Outside door

(Offstage kitchen)
Water pitcher
Water glasses
Ice
Serving plate and scones
Serving plates and tea sandwiches
Serving plates and creme puffs
Teapot
Large tray or serving cart

MUSIC USE NOTE

Licensees are solely responsible for obtaining formal written permission from copyright owners to use copyrighted music in the performance of this play and are strongly cautioned to do so. If no such permission is obtained by the licensee, then the licensee must use only original music that the licensee owns and controls. Licensees are solely responsible and liable for all music clearances and shall indemnify the copyright owners of the play(s) and their licensing agent, Samuel French, against any costs, expenses, losses and liabilities arising from the use of music by licensees. Please contact the appropriate music licensing authority in your territory for the rights to any incidental music.

IMPORTANT BILLING AND CREDIT REQUIREMENTS

If you have obtained performance rights to this title, please refer to your licensing agreement for important billing and credit requirements.

www.ingramcontent.com/pod-product-compliance
Lightning Source LLC
Chambersburg PA
CBHW052000290426
44110CB00015B/2319